I0605715

# WE DRIVE Tanker Trucks

Ruby Tuesday Books

Alix Wood

Published in 2025 by Ruby Tuesday Books Ltd.



Editors: Ruth Owen & Mark J. Sachner
Design: Alix Wood
Production: John Lingham

Photo credits:
Alamy: 14B (Therisa Stack), 18T (Jochen Tack), 18B (Sheralee Stoll), 19B (Jaromir Chalabala); iStockPhoto: 10T (Ron & Patty Thomas), 14T (ivanastar), 21 (aapsky); Shutterstock: Cover (Tverdokhlib), 1 (frolov__am/ Robert Kneschke), 2–3 (Naypong Studio), 4 (f.t. Photographer), 4–5 (refrina), 6T (rCarner), 6B (Mechan-ik), 7T (Miguel Perfectti), 7B (Kalabi Yau), 9 (Fredy Thuerig), 10B (Cobalt S-Elinoi), 11B (GBJSTOCK), 12T (Bogdan Vacarciuc), 13 (2A Stock), 15 (Chatchawal Phumkaew), 17T (Chatchawal Phumkaew), 17B (Tverdokhlib), 19T (Tyler Olson), 20T (Photofex__AUT), 20B (kckate16), 22C (Sanit Fuangnakhon), 22B (WildSnap), 23T (Andromeda Stock), 23B (santypan); Alix Wood: 8, 11T, 13, 16, 22T, 23.

Library of Congress Control Number: 2024948696

Print (Hardback) ISBN 978-1-78856-516-5
Print (Paperback) ISBN 978-1-78856-517-2
ePub ISBN 978-1-78856-518-9

Published in Minneapolis, MN
Printed in the United States

**www.rubytuesdaybooks.com**

# Contents

# Where does our gas come from?

We fill our cars with gas at a gas station.

But how does the gas get there?

A powerful truck with a big **fuel** tanker delivers the gas.

A fuel tanker truck can haul 400 bathtubs of gas!

The driver takes their cab to a **fuel depot** to pick up an empty tanker.

The driver carefully backs the cab toward the tanker.

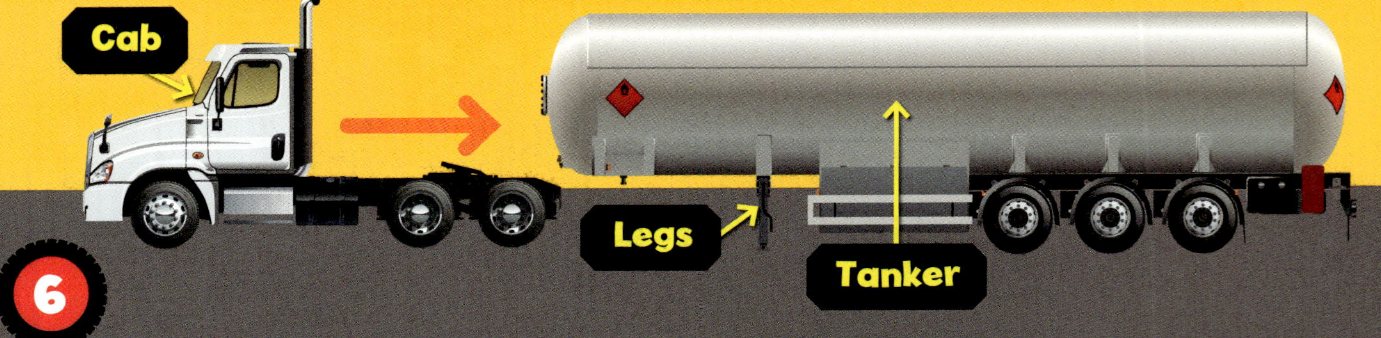

The driver hitches the cab to the tanker and connects the hoses that work the brakes.

**A tanker has legs to hold up the front end when it is parked.**

**The driver lifts the legs with this handle.**

**Leg**

The tanker is split into **compartments.**

The compartments keep the gas from sloshing back and forth.

Compartments

This makes the truck safer to drive and easier to steer.

**The tanker can deliver different types of fuel to a gas station at the same time.**

A tanker may be in an accident.

If the tanker is **damaged,** only a small amount of gas may leak from one compartment.

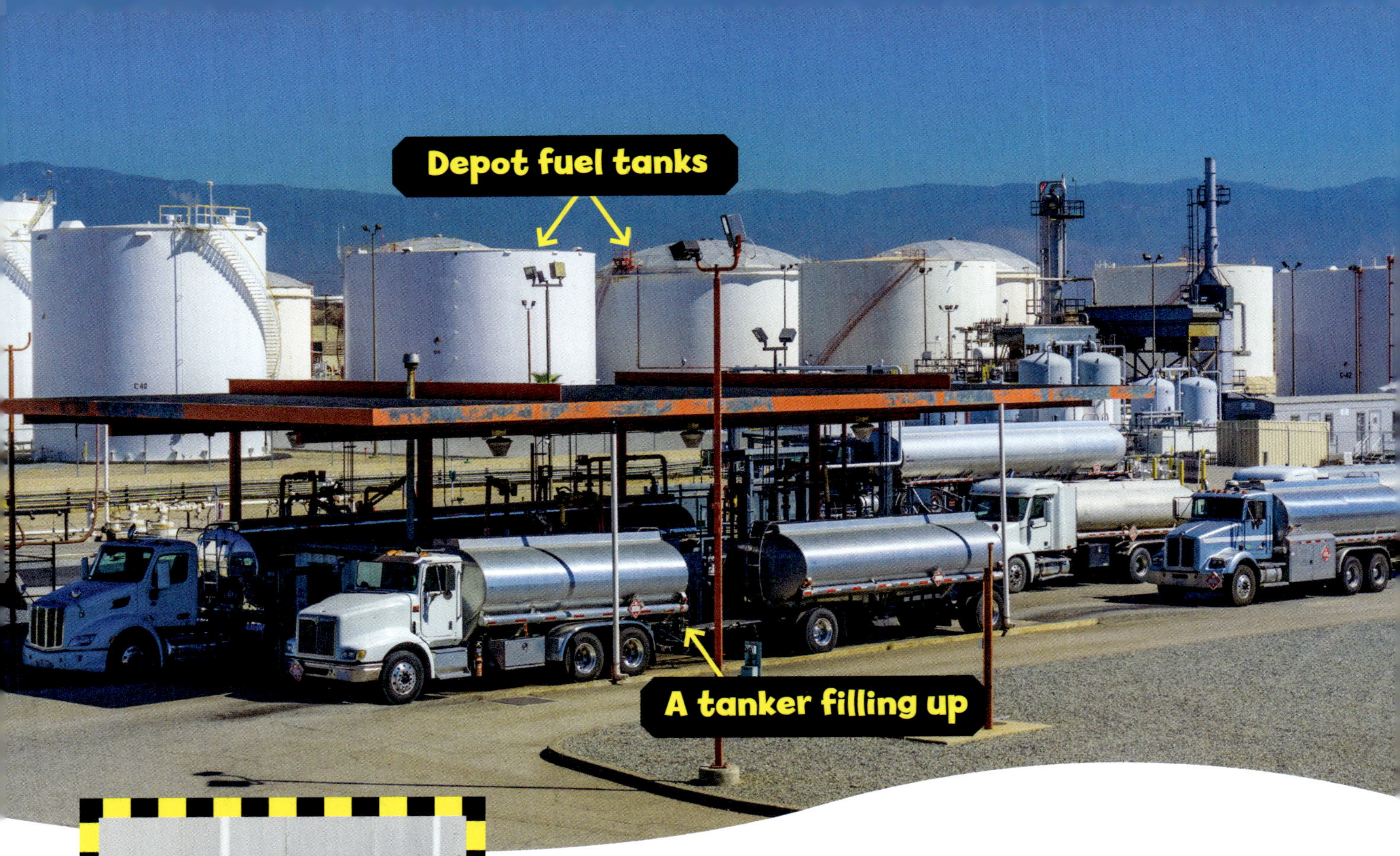
Depot fuel tanks
A tanker filling up

Hose

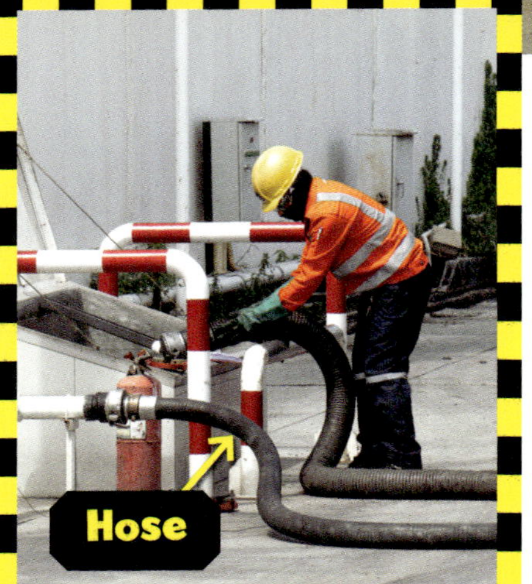

At the fuel depot, the driver fills up the tanker.

Different types of fuel flow through hoses into the tanker compartments.

As fuel flows into a tanker, a dangerous gas called **fuel vapor** is sucked out.

The driver checks the map.

Let's deliver some fuel!

Fuels, such as gasoline, can easily catch fire.

A special sign on the truck shows firefighters the truck is carrying gasoline.

A driver cleans up small fuel spills with aluminum tools that won't make sparks.

A spark might set the fuel on fire.

The tanker truck arrives at the gas station.

The gas station has big underground tanks.

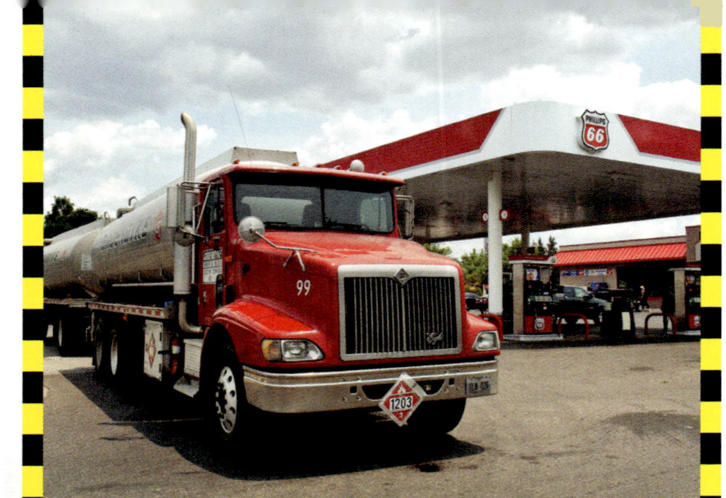

66
99
1203

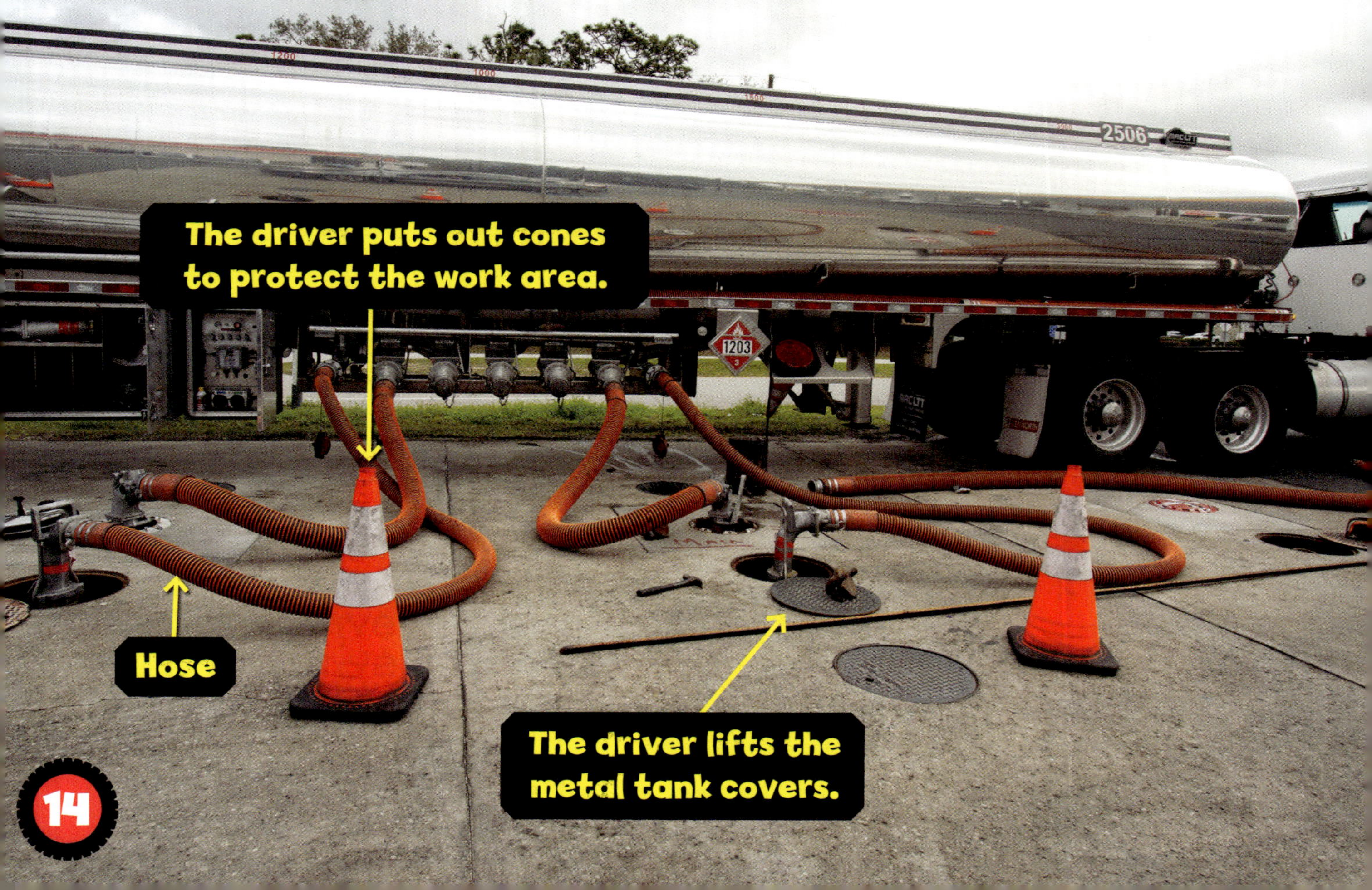
2506
1203
The driver puts out cones to protect the work area.
Hose
The driver lifts the metal tank covers.

The driver attaches the tanker's hoses to the underground tanks.

Hose

A bucket to catch drips

Then each hose is connected to the correct tanker compartment.

The driver starts the tanker's **pump.**

Fuel flows down the hose into the underground tank.

All the fuel has been delivered.

The driver disconnects the hoses and puts them back on the truck.

The driver heads back to the depot.

Another driver is leaving the fuel depot.

This time they have a tanker full of jet fuel!

Jet fuel is a special fuel used by planes.

The plane's fuel tanks are in its wings.

The driver has to climb a ladder to reach.

The driver connects a hose to the plane's tank and fills it with jet fuel.

Some airports have big underground fuel tanks.

A truck connects the underground tank to a plane's wing with a hose.

Some planes park far from the underground tanks.

A fuel tanker must deliver jet fuel to these planes.

Tanker drivers help planes and cars go on their way!

# Glossary

**compartment**
A separate part of a structure or container.

**damaged**
Broken or spoiled so a thing no longer works properly.

**fuel**
A substance such as coal, gas, or oil that is burned to produce heat or power.

**fuel depot**
A place where large amounts of fuel are stored until they are needed.

Vapor

**fuel vapor**
A type of dangerous gas that floats in the air. Fuel vapor can catch fire.

**pump**
A piece of machinery that moves a liquid from one place to another.

# Index